BRITAIN

IN OLD PHOTOGR

IRISH MANCHESTER

ALAN KEEGAN

SUTTON PUBLISHING

Sutton Publishing Limited
Phoenix Mill · Thrupp · Stroud
Gloucestershire · GL5 2BU

First published 2004

Reprinted 2004

Title page photograph: A night out at the
Ardri, late 1960s.

British Library Cataloguing in Publication Data
A catalogue record for this book is available from the
British Library.

ISBN 0-7509-3663-0

Typeset in 10.5/13.5 Photina.
Typesetting and origination by
Sutton Publishing Limited.
Printed and bound in England by
J.H. Haynes & Co. Ltd, Sparkford.

*This book is dedicated
to the memory
of Felix P. Keegan*

I would like to express what a great idea *Irish
Manchester* is. I'm only surprised it hasn't been done
before now. Good luck to Alan and his labour of love.
My mother was from County Donegal and it was
with a strong Irish background that I was born and
raised in Scotland. Moving to Manchester in the early
1960s from Celtic to play for Manchester United, I
was to enjoy, and still do, the spirit of the Manchester
Irish community.

Paddy Crerand

CONTENTS

The Manchester Martyrs' Memorial, St Joseph's Cemetery, Moston, which was unveiled in 1897.

INTRODUCTION

T his book is a celebration of the contribution the Irish have made to twentieth-century Britain and in particular to Manchester. There are many contributory factors. Construction, buildings, sport, music, language and religion are some of them. However, this is not an attempt at a comprehensive or academic analysis of the contribution the Irish have made to Manchester; rather it is a series of selective images to give a taste of what lies there, ready to be enjoyed, and to show the cultural difference the Irish have made.

Compiling *Irish Manchester* has been a labour of love. I make no apologies for this book's revel in sheer nostalgia. Some images will be familiar and some beyond recall, but the book is a timely reminder, as so much has changed.

I was born in Manchester, the youngest of five children to Felix and Margaret Keegan. It is without doubt that I must thank my family for the wonderful Irish upbringing and memories that I have been given. It couldn't have been anything else but an Irish experience, being raised in a household where I was the only member born in England. I have always been proud of being born in Manchester, but more importantly of being able to identify with my Irish heritage.

My father Felix left Ireland and came to work in the north of England (Leeds) in the late 1950s as a labourer in the construction industry and was joined in the early part of 1960 by my mother Margaret and their four children – Maura, Madge, Seamus and Padraig. They had friends in Manchester and decided to move there when the opportunity of work and 'the Start' with Murphy Construction came up for Dad. Mum had always worked in a local shop near Fenagh in County Leitrim called 'Kelly's', which sold food and general groceries, so it must have been destiny when a general grocer's shop came up for sale on Hathersage Road in Chorlton-on-Medlock, Longsight, in late 1961.

The Keegan family moved into their new home in 1962 with a new member, baby Alan. I would like to acknowledge and thank the late Tommy and May Nolan, who guided Mum and Dad in the right direction during the purchase of Hathersage Road. It was they who negotiated with the landlords about the purchase price and introduced them to the bank to obtain a loan of £1,800. They were great friends and will never be forgotten by the Keegan family.

No. 18 Hathersage Road was the foundation of my Irish childhood memories, as I grew up in an environment that was as near as it gets to living in Ireland. My family was Irish, the majority of the community were Irish, and this meant that most of the customers who came into the shop were Irish. Dad continued to work on the building sites while Mum ran the shop. Fr Willie Fallon, who was the assistant priest at the time to Fr Cavanagh in St Joseph's Church on Plymouth Grove, maintained that if you needed any information about where to get a flat or who to see for work, call into Keegan's shop. It was the focal point for all the (Irish) news in the area. He called it Radio Longsight. I know for a fact that Mum helped many Irish people who first came over to Manchester in the early days. She never forgot the help that the Nolans had given her and Dad when they first arrived.

For a young boy growing up, Hathersage Road was a vibrant, exciting place to live. It had a strong Irish community. The local church, St Joseph's, was well supported, and the local school, St Joseph's, was a great place to be. Most of us will never forget the headmistress, Miss Flynn. Every child in the area learned to swim at High Street Baths, or Victoria Baths, as it was also known. Many Irish labourers also used the Turkish Baths after a hard week working on the site.

The summer holidays couldn't come quickly enough for me, for I would spend the six weeks in County Leitrim with my aunts and uncles. I would finish school on the Friday and get the boat from Liverpool on the Saturday, spending eight hours travelling to Ireland and then two-and-a-half hours in the car to Leitrim. The memories are endless: no running water – it was so much fun going to the well for the buckets of water; no gas fire; collecting the turf for the fire – I still love the smell of burning turf now; sleeping in a bedroom that was pitch black with no street lamp outside to make you feel safe – you'd lie there thinking that you were the only person alive on the planet. You could hear every sound outside from miles around; there was no passing traffic twenty-four hours a day, as at Hathersage Road. When I look back now I can't believe that I didn't see or watch television for six weeks, but I wasn't bored for a minute, there was so much to do from morning until night: feeding the chickens, pigs, calves, milking the cows, and the thrill of learning to drive the tractor to bring in the hay.

Once back in Manchester I'd share the whole experience with my Irish brothers and sisters, thinking that they had never been part of that world. The combination of those holidays and the upbringing that I was experiencing gave me the foundation of understanding where I came from and more importantly an appreciation of the Irish way of life. (It is my belief that the majority of Irish have always worked hard to give their children the opportunities that they themselves never had: a better quality of life.)

The Carousel dance hall (formerly the Astoria dance hall) was just around the corner on Plymouth Grove. I could never understand why I couldn't go with my brothers and sisters to listen to the bands and dance the night away; after all I was eight years of age! Everyone always seemed to meet at our house and get ready for the big night out. Maura and Madge would have all their friends getting ready in the back bedroom. Seamus and Padraig would have more mates staying over in the attic bedroom. I loved it when their friends stayed over as I would always get a financial treat in the morning – it was their way of softening Mum.

I'm a great believer that in life certain things happen for a reason. In 1980, for my eighteenth birthday, Mum and Dad bought me my first set of disco equipment, which gave me the opportunity to earn some extra money. The only condition was that I played Irish music on my gigs. Once I had established a reputation as someone who did Irish gigs, I never looked back. It was this interest in Irish music and entertainment that led me to hear that the BBC had given the Irish community its own Irish radio show: Eamonn O'Neal was starting a new show called *Come into the Parlour*. I became part of the original broadcasting team and eventually left to present a radio show on Sunset Radio, also aimed at the Irish community, called *How's the Craic*. I am also very proud of the fact that I set up four restricted service radio licences that gave the Irish their own voice for twenty-eight days, twenty-four hours a day. It was known as Manchester Irish Radio.

Over the years I have had the pleasure of meeting and interviewing many Irish people through my role as a broadcaster. This has enabled me to keep in touch with my Irish roots and has given me an understanding of what it was like to come to a different country and integrate into a different way of life.

This is not meant to be an academic journal. It has been extremely difficult deciding what to include. But I hope you enjoy sharing the memories of what the Irish have contributed to Manchester.

1

Construction & Building

P. Fahey & Sons – trucks in front of Manchester Town Hall.

The hospital for injured workers, Manchester Ship Canal, 1889.

Concrete mixer on the Manchester Ship Canal, 1889–90.

Above: Workmen on Minshull Street Bridge over the Rochdale Canal, Manchester, 1905.

Workmen laying the concrete at St Anthony's Church, Wythenshawe, 1959–60.

Labourers from the Trafford Park Estates Department.

A travel permit card belonging to Edward Beirne in 1945. (Beirne had been born on 14 January 1908 in County Roscommon.)

Building site including shops and maisonettes looking north-east. Wythenshawe, Greenbrow Road, Newall Green, 1950.

Workers on the Carrington power station, 1950, including W. Ellis, A. Turner, J.F. Taylor, A. Walker and C. Baker.

John Rogers, Dusty Mills and Pat Sweeney working on the tunnel contract at Sale Moor, 1957.

Below: Baths and wash-houses at Victoria Baths, High Street (Hathersage Road), 1905.

Above: Ford Merlin engines during the Second World War.

The workforce leaving Metro Vickers, 1950s.

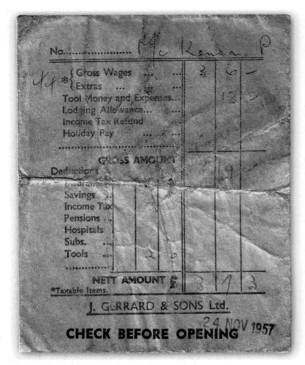
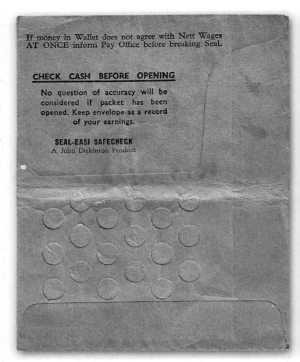

Wageslip of Patrick McKenna, 24 November 1957.

Workmen from Victor Blagden, Manchester, 1959, including Mick Moore, Tommy Quirke, John Moore and Denis Murphy.

An outing to Blackpool for the workers on the Manchester town centre job, Sunley, 1961. Pat Sweeney (third row back on the aisle) and Packie Farnan (fifth row on the right) with work colleagues, looking forward to a day out.

Kavanagh & Mannion Ltd was started in about 1964 in Manchester by Joe Kavanagh and Sean Mannion. The business is still trading from its original premises on Redgate Lane, Longsight. The young boy standing on the lorry is Andy Murphy.

Above: The first head office of what was then Joseph Kennedy & Co. Ltd, situated on the Longford Trading Estate, Stretford, 1964.

Kennedy Construction on a job in Allerton in the late 1980s. Note the name Lord Mayo on the statue (County Mayo was where Joseph Kennedy grew up).

Paddy Curley (managing director of Kennedy Construction) examines the inside of a giant bucket at a machine/plant exhibition.

A machine from P.P. O'Connor Ltd knocking down the old club house at Old Bedians playing fields, 1993.

Established in 1946, P. McGuinness & Co. Ltd is a family business that has become one of the largest and most highly respected demolition and dismantling firms in the North-West. Here it is seen clearing Cross Street near Market Street after the 1996 IRA bomb. The bomb had a devastating effect on the city centre of Manchester, as well as the Manchester Irish community – this was one part of being Irish in Manchester that the community was not proud of.

Below: Cross Street near Market Street after the rebuild, showing the walkway between the Arndale Centre and Marks & Spencer.

Finchport Ltd was set up in the 1970s by Seamus Keegan. Here we see Pat Keegan on a site in Altrincham, Sinderland Road, which was a development by Poco Homes.

Jimmy Doyle of Heyrod Construction, seen here driving the machine, 1993.

A Chartrange machine loading a truck on the new road at the Mancunian Way, 1995.

Jimmy Kennedy writes

Chartrange Ltd was established in 1985 by Mrs Mary Kennedy and her five sons as a waste haulier, operating with six lorries from premises in Ardwick, Manchester. Seeing the need to diversify, around 1989 the company began to carry out bulk excavation works as well as the haulage operations. The company has carried out a number of prestige contracts, such as the Mancunian Way and the City of Manchester Stadium, working in association with several 'Blue Chip' clients. Mary Kennedy passed away in May 1998. The business continues under the guidance of her sons.

Della Costello seen here at the controls of a JCB belonging to her husband Michael.

The construction of the City of Manchester Stadium, home of Manchester City Football Club, 2002–3. Many Irish construction companies worked on the construction of both the Commonwealth Stadium and the City of Manchester Stadium.

2

Workers & Jobs

Kelloggs factory, Mosley Road, Trafford Park, 1970s.

Mary Butler and workfriends at Kellogg's, 1972. Front row, left to right: Sadie, Mary Butler and Mary Jennings. Back row: Angela Murphy, Lily Sarsfield, the late Mary Dexter, Alice, Winnie, Norma, June and

Kellogg's food review with Tommy Galvin, 1984.

Above: Bus conductor John Morris, 1957.
Left: Two Irishmen from the same street in Dundalk serving in the Cheshire County Fire Brigade, 1966. Leading Fireman Paddy Moore, ex-Chairman of the Manchester County Louth Association (on the left) with Assistant Divisional Officer John O. McGeough.

Members of the Catholic Nurses' Guild walking in Whit Walks, 1963. These five were from Park Hospital, Davyhulme: Rita Gorman, Sheila Walsh (née McManaman), Catherine McDonald (née Mullarkey), Eileen Tupling (née McGloughlin) and Roberta Coyne.

Maureen Nash from Dromintee, South Armagh, seen here in her grocer's shop, with Corkman John O'Connor, 1976.

Maureen Nash writes:

I came to Manchester in 1953 and worked for a while at Ancoats Hospital as a cook. I then went to work for my uncle, Pat Nash, who was the manager of the Plymouth Grove Hotel. Then I bought a grocer's shop in Plymouth Street, Chorlton-on-Medlock. Later I moved to West Didsbury and had another grocer's shop on Burton Road.

I used to go to the Astoria for dancing; also the Savoy. Pierce Coogan used to run the dance hall at the Astoria. I am now retired and give a lot of my spare time to the Armagh Association.

Padraig and Alan Keegan with their father, Felix, standing outside their general grocer's shop on Hathersage Road, Chorlton-on-Medlock. Margaret (Dotie) Keegan had a general grocer's shop at 18 Hathersage Road, Longsight (High Street, near the Victoria Baths), from 1962 until 1973.

Felix and Dotie Keegan with customer Tom Moore, early 1970s.

Margaret Burke (from Cloone, County Leitrim), after many years involved in the running of the Tara Club and at an age when most people think of retiring, bought a shop on Claremont Road in Moss Side near Manchester City Football Club when she was 65 years young!

Carmoor Road Garage, Longsight. Pat Rafter, the owner, came over to England in 1962. He worked and traded in All Saints, Old Trafford, Red Bank, Longsight and Cheetham Hill. He first set up in Carmoor Road in December 1982.

UK & Ireland Insurance Services. This was the first office opened by James Wrynne and Dermot McMorrow at 531 Wilmslow Road, Withington. They have since moved to Old Lloyd's Chambers, 139 Manchester Road, Altrincham, Cheshire.

The second
Birch Lane
Garage.

Paul and Robert Griffin write:

Michael Griffin arrived in England from Ballymoe in County Galway in 1954 after serving his time as a mechanic in his home town in the business called Flanagan's, which doubled as a funeral directors and general store.

On his arrival in Manchester he worked at Rootes, which became known as Tom Garner's. In 1960 he set up his own garage at Birch Lane in Longsight (hence the name Birch Lane Garage), specialising in mechanical and body repairs. In the early years he had contracts with many large Irish construction and demolition companies (Connell & Finnegan, Kavanagh & Mannion to name but two).

As time progressed Birch Lane Garage developed a site on Clarence Road in Longsight, which sold vehicle salvage and spares. In 1980, because of expansion, it moved to larger premises in Pond Street, City Road, near Deansgate, ironically a stone's throw from the old Rootes site. Again, because of expansion, in 1990, Birch Lane Garage had to move to its present site on Textile Street, West Gorton.

Michael Griffin was active in the company until his death in late 2003 at the age of 76. Michael's sons, Paul and Robert Griffin, now run the business.

P. Fahey & Sons Ltd, Globe House, 92 Chorlton Road. Left to right: Andrew, Simon, Patrick (founder) and Peter Fahey. It was the late Patrick Fahey, who originated from County Mayo, who founded the company in the 1950s. From its storage and distribution facility in Old Trafford, the company is currently run by third-generation family members, Andrew and Simon Fahey, and their father, Peter. 'When Patrick Fahey set up the removals business, it was a very basic affair,' commented Peter Fahey. 'He bought an old hand cart from a second-hand shop and made his own trailer, offering a removals service in the Old Trafford area. By adhering to his basic principles, however, we have managed to build the business over three generations into a thriving concern.'

'Any Time is Travel Time with Aran', 1986. Kevin Moran officially opens the new Aran Travel Shop, 1068 Chester Road, Stretford. Jim and Kathleen Phelan, along with Jim and Bridie Galvin, are seen here with staff and friends. Left to right: Kevin Curry, Martin Flynn, Kath Phelan, Bridie Galvin, Terry Jordan, Jim Phelan, Eimear Phelan, James Phelan, Kevin Moran, Margaret Curry, Michael Galvin, Tom Galvin, Patricia Frainey and Pat Frainey. Ten years later Aran Travel won the Stena Line award for ferrying more Stena passengers than any other independent travel agent.

'Travel the Wall's Way'. For many years Michael Wall organised travel back home to Ireland from Manchester.

'Ireland by B & I'. Margaret Curry and friends at the launch of a new B & I ferry. Over the years many travel agents have catered for the needs of the Irish community: Broadleys Travel in Levenshulme, the Irish Travel Bureau in Sale, and the Irish Travel Centre in the Irish World Heritage Centre.

CONNECTING TRAINS (Weekdays)

FROM	DEP.	ARRIVE LIVERPOOL	
Birmingham (Snow Hill) ...	4.41 p.m.	Birkenhead (W.)	*7.50 p.m.
" (New St.)	6.05 p.m.	Lime St.	8.49 p.m.
Bournemouth (West) ... A	9.20 a.m.	Birkenhead (W.)	5.41 p.m.
" (Cent.) ... A	9.30 a.m.	Birkenhead (W.)	5.41 p.m.
Bradford (Exchange) ...	5.08 p.m.	Exchange	7.33 p m.
Bristol (Temple Meads) ...	2.05 p.m.	Lime St.	7.20 p m.
Cardiff (General)	2.05 p.m.	Lime St.	7.20 p.m.
		Birkenhead (W.)	*7.50 p.m.
Halifax	5.35 p.m.	Exchange	7.33 p.m.
Harrogate	4.23 p.m.	Lime St.	7.52 p.m.
Huddersfield	5.55 p.m.	Lime St.	7.52 p.m.
Hull (Paragon)	4.00 p.m.	Lime St.	7.52 p.m.
LEEDS (City)	5.20 p.m.	Lime St. ...	7.52 p.m.
Leicester (London Road) ...	4.17 p.m.	Central	8.24 p.m.
LONDON (Paddington) ...	2.10 p.m.	Birkenhead (W.)	*7.50 p.m.
" (Euston) ...	4.30 p.m.	Lime St.	8.27 p.m.
MANCHESTER (Central) ...	7.30 p.m.	Central	8.24 p.m.
" (Exchange)	7.01 p.m.	Lime St.	7.52 p.m.
" (Victoria) ...	6.45 p.m.	Exchange	7.33 p.m.
Newcastle-on-Tyne (Central)	12.51 p.m.	Exchange	7.33 p.m.
Northampton (Castle) ...	5.15 p.m.	Lime St.	8.27 p.m.
Norwich (Thorpe)	10.56 a.m.	Central	7.27 p.m.
Nottingham (City)	4.12 p.m.	Central	8.24 p.m.
Oxford (W.R.)	2.38 p.m.	Birkenhead (W.)	*7.50 p.m.
Plymouth North Road) ...	8.45 a.m.	Birkenhead (W.)	6.35 p.m.
" " ...	10.25 a.m.	Lime St.	7.20 p m.
Preston	7.18 p.m.	Exchange	8.28 p.m.
Reading (West)	1.56 p.m.	Birkenhead (W.)	7.50 p.m.
Sheffield (City)	4.30 p.m.	Central	8.24 p.m.
" (Victoria) ...	4.24 p.m.	Central	7.27 p.m.
Southampton (Central) ... A	10.33 a.m.	Birkenhead (W.)	5.41 p.m.
Stoke-on-Trent	6.28 p.m.	Lime St.	8.27 p.m.
Wolverhampton (Low Level)	5.09 p.m.	Birkenhead (W.)	*7.50 p.m.
" High Level)	6.41 p.m.	Lime St.	8.49 p.m.
Worcester (Shrub Hill) ...	2.35 p.m.	Birkenhead (W.)	*7.50 p.m.
York	3.10 p.m.	Exchange	7.33 p.m.

Opposite and above: B & I Line Travel information brochure, 1950–1.

PASSENGER FARES TO DUBLIN

	SINGLE			RETURN (VALID ONE MONTH)		
FROM	1st Class on Vessel and 1st Class Rail	1st Class on Vessel and 3rd Class Rail	3rd Class	1st Class on Vessel and 1st Class Rail	1st Class on Vessel and 3rd Class Rail	3rd Class
	£ s. d.	£ s. d.	£ s. d.	£ s. d.	£ s. d.	£ s. d.
LIVERPOOL	1 17 9	—	17 3	*3 6 1	—	*1 11 7
BIRMINGHAM	3 12 3	2 16 9	1 18 11	5 13 5	4 17 6	3 1 3
BRISTOL	4 16 4	3 11 4	2 15 3	7 6 11	5 15 6	4 3 2
LEEDS	3 10 2	2 15 7	1 16 8	5 9 5	4 17 2	2 19 7
LONDON	5 8 9	3 18 8	3 0 4	7 16 7	6 6 10	4 9 8
MANCHESTER	2 16 5	2 8 2	1 8 2	4 12 4	4 3 9	2 8 2
NOTTINGHAM	3 14 3	2 18 0	2 2 0	6 0 0	4 18 10	3 6 6

CHILDREN OVER 3 YEARS AND UNDER 14 YEARS—HALF FARE.

*RETURN FARES LIVERPOOL AND DUBLIN VALID 3 MONTHS.

THROUGH FARES WITH ALL PRINCIPAL STATIONS

TRANSFER Third Class to First Class on Vessel—24/2 Single, 40/1 Return (on Through Fares)

Passenger's Luggage up to 150 lbs. (1st Class) and 100 lbs. (3rd Class) carried free.

Curry Travel Services, 139 Wilbraham Road, Fallowfield, 1980s. Margaret Curry had been involved in the Irish travel industry for many years before setting up her own business.

Margaret Curry writes:

Before 1970 there were two ways to travel to Ireland from Manchester. You could fly with Aer Lingus, which had a reservation office at 67 Deansgate, to Dublin or Shannon. The only other way home was the boat train. I remember that you could purchase tickets from Manchester's main station, which in those days was Victoria. The boat train journey took you from Victoria station to Crewe, where you changed for Holyhead. When the train arrived at Holyhead station, it pulled up beside the mail boat, either the *Princess Maud* or the *Canberra*.

3

Pubs & Clubs

Billy and Marie Murphy with John and Lily White, June 1951.
This photograph was taken at The Killarney Social Club, 32a Stretford Road
(above Burton's), All Saints, Manchester.

Aunty's Bar public house on Oxford Road, 1958. Many Irishmen were given a 'start' in Aunty's Bar.

Paddy Moore writes:

Situated in Oxford Road was a men-only public house called Aunty's Bar, this was the first port of call for many a young Irishman who had just arrived. Here he would get an address to find digs and details of how to go about finding a job and getting a 'start'.

Along with a few fellow Irishmen I joined the City of Manchester Fire Brigade and in our off-duty times, especially on a Sunday night, we would do a pub tour. Starting in Aunty's Bar, we would make our way to the Gog and Magog in Ardwick, then continue to the Brunswick in Brunswick Street, then to the Grafton, and last of all the College. All of the pubs had an Irish clientele and at closing time it was straight to Sharrocks dance hall, situated at the Oxford Road end of Brunswick Street. This hall was the mecca for young Irish people on a Sunday night and many a match was made there especially with young Irish nurses from the nearby Manchester Royal Infirmary.

The old Chorlton Masonic Hall/Chorlton Social and Bowling Club, 17 High Lane, Chorlton, 1959.

A recent picture of the Irish Association Social Club, 17 High Lane, Chorlton.

Paul Costello and colleagues write:

'It's time we ran our own do.'

That was the remark that sowed the seed that later gave birth to the Irish Association Club. It was made by the late John Donelon to Tom Finnigan in the cloakroom of the Alma Lodge Hotel, Stockport Road, when they and some of their friends were leaving the hotel after a Catenian dinner and dance in 1951. They had hoped to get a drink at the hotel bar when the dinner dance was over, but it had gone time, and all the bars were closed. Four more years had to pass before the birth of the association took place, but the idea was constantly discussed whenever a few of the Irish lads met after a night out.

During the following four years many members of the Irish community in Manchester had become self-employed independent businessmen. Some of them had joined the Catenians, and some had joined the Knights of St Columba. They attended the annual social functions arranged by these two bodies, but because they lived in different parts of the city these were almost the only times in the year when they, and their wives, met socially. One Sunday evening in late 1955, after many discussions about clubs and meeting places, five or six of the Irish lads who lived in the south of Manchester met in the Knights of St Columba's Club in Princess Road. Tom Finnigan suggested that it was about time the Irish community in Manchester had at least an annual dance at Christmas time, as every other national group except the Irish had something. This suggestion caught on immediately, and the very next week the group found a regular meeting place in a city centre pub called the Mill Stone, run by Paddy O'Malley, a very keen supporter of the group.

At the very first meeting, which took place in the Conference Room of the Mill Stone, the group, after long and serious discussion, decided that henceforth it would be known as the 'Irish Association' (as suggested by Michael McKeown), and Martin Flynn was elected the first chairman. The affairs of the meetings were conducted in a most business-like manner, and a date in early January 1956 was fixed for the dinner dance, to be held in the Grand Hotel. This was the first big social occasion of the Irish Association and an annual dinner dance has been held ever since.

Martin Flynn, as previously mentioned, was the chairman, Tom Finnigan the secretary and the late George Hyland the master of ceremonies. One of the guests that evening was Alderman Leslie Lever MP. He arrived late for the meal because he had been attending a meeting of the City Council where he had been chosen Lord Mayor Elect for the following year. Mr Lever, who subsequently became Lord Lever, remained a staunch friend of the Irish Association until his death. Bishop Beck also befriended the association from the very start. He came to the dinner dances every year and he always came to, and enjoyed, the functions that came to be known as the 'Day After' the dance. It was he who suggested that the association invite the Irish bishops to the dinner dances. (The first to accept was Bishop Staunton of Wexford.)

In late 1959 there had been a rumour that the Freemasons wanted to sell privately their premises at 17 High Lane, Chorlton. The club was bought for £4,500. The purchase price of the club was raised almost entirely by contributions in the form of interest-free loans, from the founding members, Messrs M. Connell, J. O'Grady, J. Beirne, J. Donelon, A. Cafferty, T. Finnigan, M. Flynn, M. O'Dwyer, M. McKeown and J. Dowd. A trading account was opened with the National Bank, Moseley Street, where most of the members banked. A bank overdraft and mortgage had to be arranged, because considerable sums, over and above the purchase price, were going to be needed for repairs and new furniture. All the above members had to act as guarantors for this bank loan and mortgage: Messrs Connell, Finnigan, O'Dwyer and O'Grady for the bank loan and Messrs McKeown, Flynn, Cafferty and Donelon for the mortgage. The National Bank wasn't taking too many risks!

The rear (main) entrance to the Irish Association Social Club.

The Irish Association Social Club Dinner Dance at the Grand Hotel, 1963. The top table includes Monsignor Sewell, Bishop Thomas Holland, Mr and Mrs John Donelon and Mr and Mrs Martin Flynn.

Opposite: The Lally family, all of whom have been involved in the running of the club since 1982. Left to right: Anthony Lally, Ann Mulligan, Kathleen Fisher, Margaret Fox (licensee), Martin Lally, Myra Lally and Michael Fox.

Early members of the Irish Association Social Club on the stairs of the Grand Hotel, 1963. Front row, left to right: Martin Flynn, Paddy Boyle, Bishop Burke, Fr Casey, Monsignor Sewell, John Kane and Jimmy Hammett. Other members include John Dowd, Tony Deacy, Michael Connell, Pat McKelvey, Micky Finn, John Kennedy, Michael Maloney, Tom Flaherty, Victor Leyden, Tony Deacy, Paddy Curley, Fr Michael Hoare, Fr John Laide, Tom Finnigan, Jimmy Benson, Joe Kennedy, Fr Jim Ryan, Tom Connor, Fr Curristan, Fr Dave O'Kane, Tom Neylon, Jim O'Grady, Fr Brendan Quilter and Paddy Curley.

Opposite: St John's parish centre, Chequers Road, Chorlton. This was the original St John's School.

Irish Association committee members, seen here with Monsignor Sewell, standing at the Manchester Martyrs' Memorial in St Joseph's Cemetery, Moston, early 1960s.

The Clarence, Wilmslow Road, Rusholme.

St Edward's Confraternity Club, Great Western Street, 1961.

Above: The Fallowfield, Wilbraham Road, Fallowfield, 1973.

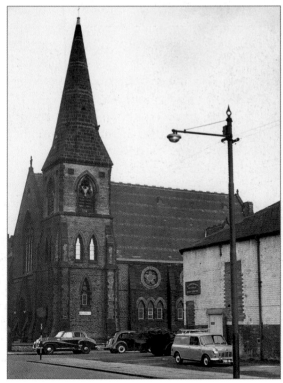

St Lawrence's Catholic Church, City Road, Hulme, near Chester Road, 1962.

St Brendan's Catholic Irish Centre, City Road, Hulme, 1962.

Michael Sheehan writes:

Monday 13 June 1960. The place – the club rooms at All Saints, Manchester. The occasion – the first meeting of the committee of St Brendan's Irish Centre. Present at the meeting a young priest from Derry, Fr Emmet Fullen. He is representing the GAA. The chairman, Mr Ansbro, welcomes him.

Fr Dorran announces that the Lyceum Cinema at City Road has been purchased. It is a new home for St Brendan's, but a good deal of work remains to be done. £10,000 has to be raised to cover the cost of reconstruction. There is an air of confidence that the target can be reached once the centre sets about catering for the 'spiritual, social welfare and entertainment' needs of the Irish community.

Every Irish person in Manchester knows how well St Brendan's succeeded over the years in fulfilling the objectives identified that night in 1960.

St Brendan's has always been a caring place, somewhere to find a sympathetic ear and practical help in relation to accommodation and employment. That's something that has been invaluable to thousands of newcomers to the city. St Brendan's has always been a place that feels like home, a place to see familiar faces and hear familiar voices. It has a warmth that has eased the pain of separation from Ireland for so many. It has a certain dignity that comes from fostering our national culture – Irish music, song and dance; the Irish language; Irish sports, pastimes and crafts. St Brendan's has helped to make us proud of what we are.

St Brendan's has never been an exclusive place. It has been a place for relaxation, enjoyment and entertainment for all. It's been caring. It's had warmth. It's had pride in Irish identity. It's never been pretentious. Where do these qualities come from? There can only be one answer. That young priest from Derry, who attended the first meeting in 1960, and went on to become Director of St Brendan's for fifteen years. He stamped his own character on St Brendan's – a character that epitomises Christian virtue. We Irish in Manchester have much to thank him for.

Fr Fullen seen here with Harry Purcell.

Canon A. Doran writes:

Father Hugh Emmet Fullen (1934–85) was born at Longfield, Desertmartin, South Derry, in 1934, the youngest of a large family. He attended the local parish school before going on to St Colum's College, Derry, for his secondary education. In 1952 he entered All Hallows College, Dublin, and offered himself for service in the Diocese of Salford. Having graduated with an honours Classics degree, he was ordained priest at All Hallows College in June 1959.

Having served for short periods in Pendlebury and New Moston, he was appointed assistant priest at St Augustine's, Chorlton-on-Medlock, a busy parish in the heart of Manchester. After five years there, he was appointed to St Mary's, Mulberry Street, followed by two other appointments at St Dunstan's, Moston, and St Mary's, Denton. In 1980 he was appointed Parish Priest of St Lawrence's, Old Trafford, with care of St Brendan's Diocesan Catholic Irish Centre. He died suddenly on 25 March 1985, the feast of the Annunciation.

From the time of his first appointment to St Augustine's, he became aware of the difficulties facing young men and women coming from Ireland for the first time. He devoted himself whole-heartedly to their welfare for the rest of his priestly life, a large portion of which was centred on St Brendan's, the legion of Mary Praesidium there, and the many and varied activities that flowed from there.

Fr Fullen was in his youth an outstanding Gaelic footballer. He and his two brothers led their club to a sensational triumph in the 1953 Derry championship. Soon afterwards, he was a regular on the Derry team and was still on the panel when Derry made sporting history by qualifying for the 1958 all-Ireland final in which they were beaten by Dublin. In Manchester, Fr Fullen maintained his involvement with the Gaelic Athletic Association (GAA) – he was the principal founder of St Lawrence's GAA Club, and as a result he received an Irish Post-B & I GAA Centenary Award in recognition of the club's multi-dimensional activities.

Opposite: Fr Emmet Fullen's memorial programme. The programme cover was designed by Paul Sheehan, who was fifteen years old at the time.

in grateful remembrance

Derry

Vita ~ Veritas ~ Victoria

Fr. Emmet Fullen
1934~85

Nº 000049

Souvenir Programme 50p

Mary Reilly and Maureen McHugh (middle of front row) with staff and friends at St Brendan's, early 1980s.

The O'Carolan committee and friends at St Brendan's, 1974. Pat Sweeney, Eddie Kiley, Margaret Curry, J.J. McTiernan and friends.

Comhaltas Ceoltoiri Eireann

Over 400 branches of Comhaltas Ceoltoiri Eireann (CCE), at home and abroad, organise and present traditional musicians, singers, and dancers in the various events promoted by the movement.

The branch is the fundamental and most important unit of the Comhaltas movement. It is the branch that makes it possible for the native cultural characteristics to be propagated and strengthened within the community. Members come together to organise sessions, classes, concerts, festivals, exhibitions, fleadhanna cheoil and other competitive events, both for their own enjoyment and for that of the community at large.

Mrs Mary O'Brien with daughter Bernie and her husband Martin White upstairs at St Brendan's in the 1980s. Notice the county plaques on the wall in the background.

Apsley Cottage, Apsley Grove, situated at the side of the Apollo Theatre, Ardwick Green, 1964. Over the years many international Irish artistes would visit the Apsley Cottage prior to a concert at the Apollo. It was run for many years by the popular Irishwoman Kath O'Malley.

St Aloysius Catholic Club (which became the 32 Club), Harkness Street, off Higher Ardwick, 1969.

The Grove Club, 250 Plymouth Grove, Longsight. The Grove was a former garage that sold specialist cars. In 1988 Galway man Michael Costello opened the club with his wife Della, who came from County Mayo. The Grove closed in 2001.

A charity football dinner at the Grove Club, with (from left to right) compère Vince Miller, Niall Quinn, Tracy Costello, Jack Charlton, Della Costello and Michael Costello, 1991.

The Albert, Wilmslow Road, Withington, 1990s. A cosy corner of Withington, owned by Tommy and Sean Grogan.

The Palace cinema, Farmside Place, off Stockport Road, Levenshulme, 1971. Walt Disney's *Aristocats* was on the bill. The cinema later became the Palace nightclub.

The Palace
nightclub,
celebrating the
Manchester Irish
Festival, 1996.

The Manchester Irish Players on stage at the Palace nightclub, Levenshulme, in *Don't Tell The Wife*, spring
1995. The photo shows Eileen O'Boye and Liam Bradshaw (who at one time had also been the manager at
St Brendan's, Old Trafford).

Plymouth Grove Hotel, Plymouth Grove, 1960s. For many years the hotel was managed by Pat Cash.

Opposite, top: The Osborne Dance Hall, 1986. The Osborne is situated on Oldham Road in Miles Platting near the city centre.

Opposite, bottom: The Clipper Showband on stage at the Osborne, 1967: Tom Ahern (accordion), Tom Coogan (drums) and Tom Owen (guitar).

English Martyrs' Parish Centre, Alexander Road South, Whalley Range, 1970s.

English Martyrs' Parish Centre

During the mid-1960s the parishioners and clergy of English Martyrs decided that it would be beneficial for the parish to have a parish centre. The allotments adjacent to the church were earmarked and the task of fund-raising began. After a period of two years of detailed planning, the parish centre opened in September 1973.

In the early years of the parish centre, the membership peaked at over 1,000 members. Over the years it has been used by many groups and organisations and English Martyrs is proud that directly and indirectly, through both individuals and the Manchester Irish associations, it has supported and helped to raise many thousand of pounds for charities such as Christies, Rainbow Trust, Pendlebury and the MS Society, along with fund-raising for individual families who for one reason or another needed help. In recent years the centre has entered floats in the annual St Patrick's Day Parade.

The original members of the English Martyrs' committee, 1973. Back row, left to right: Tommy Grogan (steward), Sean Fisher, Sean Brennan, Joe Coughlan, Brian Reid, Jack Bowes, Sean Higgins. Front row: Jimmy McNicholas, Stanley Jones, Fr Bernard Brennan, Martin Maloney, George O'Neil.

Tuesday night at St Wilfrid's, Birchvale Close, Hulme, 1965. Seen here are Frank Cummins, Fr Hoare, Paddy Feery, Jimmy Burns and friends.

The original entrance to St Kentigern's Parish Centre. The centre on Hart Road in Fallowfield was built in 1968 and, thanks to the willing volunteers, it was soon up and running under the stewardship of Roscommon man Mark Golden and the watchful eye of Fr M. Stanley and the club committee. Throughout the years it has always been a well-known venue especially with the Irish community, offering language, music, step and set dancing classes, bands and sports. In March 2002, after thirty-four years of dedicated service, Mark Golden relinquished the helm in favour of a leisurely and well-deserved retirement, handing over to another Irishman to take control, Kevin Fitzpatrick from County Fermanagh.

The Tara dance hall, Oldham Road, was started by Margaret and Patrick Burke in about 1949. Pictured here in the early 1960s are Etna, Felix, Dotie, Midge, Sunny Bohan, Margaret Burke, John Bohan and Felix Doran.

The Four Provinces Ceili Band performing at the Holy Name Social Club, All Saints. This photograph was taken at a presentation night for Comhaltas Ceoltoiri Eireann O'Carolan's branch to J.J. McTiernan (later to become Fr McTiernan), 1980s.

The College cinema (an entertainment and leisure cinema and wrestling club), Coupland Street, Chorlton-on-Medlock, 1964. It was later to become the Ardri.

The front of the New Ardri, 1980s. Tommy McKenna bought the popular Irish club from Jim Connell in 1978.

A mural on the side of the New Ardri building. Painted in 1985 by Mike Regan, this was part of his GCSE exam while studying at St Pius X High School, which was situated on Laindon Road, Victoria Park.

Tom Coogan (on the left), seen here with friends in the Ardri, early 1970s. The owner, Jim Connell (wearing the bow tie), is sitting on the right.

The Irish World Heritage Centre.

Louise Campbell and Patrick Marmion write:

The Irish World Heritage Centre was officially opened by Peter Barry, Minister of Foreign Affairs, on 2 November 1986. As well as providing a venue for Irish people to socialise and pursue Irish cultural activities it was dedicated to Irish emigrants worldwide in recognition of their achievements and the positive contribution they made wherever they settled.

The centre was created from the council of county associations (the only other similar organisation was in London at the time), which was made up of six main counties. Pat Sweeney was elected the first chairman. The emphasis was on helping the committee, with the main emphasis of establishing an Irish Centre. Before the centre, Manchester's Irish community supported up to seventeen Catholic clubs, but no Irish Centre as such.

With no money and no premises, a small sub-committee was formed to find premises for the new centre. In the end it was Michael Forde who came across the British Legion Club on Queens Road in Cheetham Hill. At the time the British Legion Club was closed, but on the market. It was vandalised and needed a large amount of work, so again with no money the decision was made to go ahead and start the centre.

The centre owes its existence to the tremendous spirit of the Irish in Manchester and the thousands of hours of voluntary labour that took a vandalised building and turned it into one of the world's leading Irish centres.

The founding members were: from Connaught: T. Mitchell, P. Feeley, M. Forde, J. Keane, P. Conway and T. Burke; from Ulster: J. McCormack, D. McGuire, P. Sweeney, P. Lambe, G. Lambe and D. Greer; from Leinster: J. Johnson, P. Browne, G. Anderson, and M. Maher; and from Munster: M. Fionn, M. Kelly, T. Ely, F. Linnane and J. Walsh.

The Banba Blarney Band, seen here with Paddy Feery and Jimmy Byrne. The club was on Queens Road, Cheetham Hill, the site where the Irish World Heritage centre is now located.

A large crowd gathered outside the Blarney Dance Hall (now the Irish World Heritage Centre), Queens Road, October 1961. They were about to embark on a day trip to Blackpool. Pictured here are Eileen Bossens, Pat Long, Kitty Donahue, Paddy White, the late Tom McNamara, Mary Dundon, Michael Dundon and Eileen McNamara.

Johnny Loughrey with his band in the Railway, Salford, 1980s. The group featured Pete Sweeney on guitar, Johnny Loughrey on guitar, Tim Bergin on drums and Paul Lacey on bass.

Johnny Loughrey writes:

I came over from Newtownstewart, County Tyrone, in the late 1960s. I met and married Mary, who originated from County Mayo. We have three children, Michelle, Paula and Shaun, and at the time of writing six grandchildren.

I started singing in Irish clubs and bars in Manchester shortly after I arrived in the UK. I joined Paddy Feery's band (the Banba Blarney Band) in the early 1970s. Paddy was from County Offaly. My career with Paddy and his band started at St Brendan's on City Road, Old Trafford; this was on a Thursday night. I was with Paddy and the band for nearly eight years.

I formed my own group in 1980 and played a regular residency in the Railway Hotel, Salford. The landlord there was Kevin Feeny from County Cork, who ran it with his wife, Julia. I was there for three years before moving to the famous Boatman's Home to play for the owner, Jim Curley from County Sligo. I was there for four years. Many famous names came into the Boatman's Home: film stars, footballers and nearly every Irish person in Manchester came in at one time or another. It was a great four years. Brilliant.

In June 1996 I gave up my day job at John Kennedy, where I had worked for twenty-eight years, and went on the road with my band full-time, touring Ireland as well as the UK, and eventually I moved to Ireland and based the band there.

The Boatman's Home, City Road, Hulme, 1973. This pub was always popular with the Irish construction contractors. The landlord was Jim Curley.

The Astoria, 34 Plymouth Grove, Chorlton-on-Medlock, 1959.

Tony Coogan writes:

My father, Pierce Coogan, was born in Manchester of Irish parents on 11 March 1908. His father, Thomas Coogan, was a tailor from Kilkenny and his mother, Margaret, a seamstress from Cork. At about the age of ten Pierce went to St Joseph's, where the Christian Brothers taught him to play the alto saxophone. This ability was to prove valuable in later years, especially when times were hard, for he was able to earn extra money by playing in dance bands. While still at St Joseph's he played in their military band, which was engaged by the town council to play in various parks on Sundays. His favourite was St Michael's, in Angel Meadow, between Style Street and Aspin Lane. There, the band always attracted a crowd, who would sometimes dance to the music.

He married Florence (Florrie or Flo) Dunn in 1934 and I was born on 22 April 1935. Dad was cleaning school windows during the day and playing sax in the evenings. By the outbreak of war in 1939 I had been joined by my brothers, Peter (1 July 1937) and Tom (19 January 1939). My father had graduated from school windows to cleaning and repairing neon signs on high buildings. This came to an end with the blackout, when all lights were switched off. He was given a job by the same firm, Claud-gen, maintaining internal telephones at A.V. Roe's aircraft factory (later British Aerospace). In this job he was exempt from military service, which, no doubt, helped him to survive the war. At the time of the Manchester blitz, when bombs fell often, my mother was expecting our sister, Florence Mary. Mollie duly arrived on 4 January 1941.

Dad was playing his sax with groups like the Apollo Band. A large bomb demolished the opposite side of our street, killing my playmate Jimmy Turner and his mother. The baby survived with only a cut lip. Our house, 35 Westmoreland Street, Harpurhey, was declared 'unsafe', having lost all windows and frames. We were rehoused at 5 Plant Hill Road, Higher Blackley – a nice three-bedroomed house on a council estate.

By 1946 Pierce was playing at an Irish club called the Adelphi. The musicians were allowed by Jack Morley, the proprietor, to open the place for dancing on Sunday afternoons. This was a minor success and gave Pierce the confidence to go into partnership with Tony Stuart, the owner of the Astoria Ballroom, when the chance came. The Astoria Irish Club opened in 1948. Initially it opened only on Sunday nights, but it was an immediate success, so Tony Stuart was only too happy to allow Saturday nights as well. Wednesday nights were charity dances. The entire profit from each Wednesday night went to a deserving cause such as someone injured at work or a priest trying to start a new parish. A large proportion of the customers were nurses from various hospitals in Manchester, Stockport, Oldham, Rochdale, Bury and Bolton. Many of these places were difficult to return to, late at night, so Pierce, always concerned for the safety of his clients, provided free transport to most of them. Every dance night coaches took people home to Didsbury, Withington Hospital, Sale and Urmston. My brother Tom drove a minibus to take people, mostly nurses, to all the hospitals on the northern side of the city. There were two resident bands: the 'modern' band, in which I played second alto sax, and the ceili band, in which my brother Tom played drums. The bands played alternately, the modern band starting the evening and ending it with the

Pierce and Florence Coogan standing at the entrance of the Astoria.

'Soldiers' Song'. Various visiting attractions appeared, such as the Jack Ruane Showband, the first Irish showband to visit England, followed by the Clipper Carltons and others. Josef Locke came several times, as did Betty Kelly's Dance Troupe and the Kerry Pipers. No alcoholic drink was sold on the premises, so 'passout' tickets were issued to allow people to visit the pub and return later.

Over the years the building's structure, particularly the roof and the dance floor, began to need attention. The owner, Tony Stuart, refused to agree to any repair work, so, very reluctantly, Pierce began to look for other premises. The Assembly Rooms in Cheetwood, a very ornate structure, had been built by the Jewish Community in 1852. It had become disused and was available to rent. The Assembly Club opened in 1961.

Although it was a success and had a licensed bar, it never enjoyed the popularity of the Astoria. When, eventually, the owner of the building gave notice that he needed it for other purposes, Pierce decided to retire.

The dance hall at the Astoria, 1948.

Irish Dance Club

GRAND OPENING NIGHT

SUNDAY, 24th OCTOBER, 1948

8 p.m. to 11 p.m.

MEMBERS 2/-   GUESTS 2/-

ALL STEP THIS WAY
START NOW TO DANCE IN COMFORT
TO THE MUSIC OF PIERCE (JACK) COOGAN AND HIS BAND
OVER THE FINEST FLOOR IN MANCHESTER
REMEMBER TO TELL ALL YOUR FRIENDS
IT IS WHAT YOU HAVE WAITED FOR
ATTEND ON OPENING NIGHT AND SEE FOR YOURSELVES

There is room for everyone so invite your Friends to the FINEST IRISH CLUB IN MANCHESTER

THE—

ASTORIA
Irish Dance
Club

PLYMOUTH GROVE,
CHORLTON-ON-MEDLOCK,
MANCHESTER.
Telephone: ARDwick 1431 and 2010

The opening promotional leaflet for the Astoria, 1948.

The Astoria doormen, 1950s: Pat Sweeney, Johnny Coen, Mick Kelly and the late Tom McGagh.

1952	HOLIDAY	DANCES	1953
CHRISTMAS		**NEW YEAR**	

WEDNESDAY, December 24th
Grand Xmas Eve Carnival
8 to 11.30   Admission 3/-

THURSDAY, December 25th
XMAS DAY
8 to 11   Admission 2/6

FRIDAY, December 26th
8 to 11.30   Admission 2/6

WEDNESDAY, December 31st
New Year Carnival
8 p.m. to 1 a.m.   Admission 3/-

THURSDAY, January 1st

8 to 11.30   Admission 2/6

Saturday and Sunday Dances as usual 8 to 11.30

Please note:—
Members who are
going to Midnight Mass please collect
their coats at 11.15 to avoid the
queue.

Pierce Coogan, the Musicians, and
the Committee wish all members
**A Merry Christmas
and a Happy New Year**

The Astoria Christmas and New Year dances list, 1952/3.

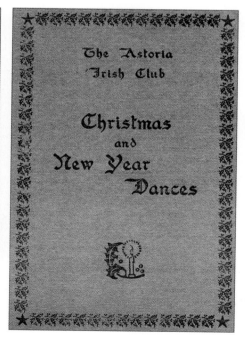

The Astoria
Irish Club

Christmas
and
New Year
Dances

The Astoria in 1965, without the railings at the front.

Below: A full dance hall, early 1950s (note the fluorescent light on the stage).

Above: The Astoria Dance Champions, 1962.
Left to right: Tony and Maureen Cagney
(runners-up), Stephen Cagney and Kathleen
Lord (winners) and Kate Coughlin.

Peggy McCabe with Tony Coogan and
Kathleen Coonan, 1956.

The Assembly Rooms, Cheetham Hill Road (corner of Derby Street), 1959. This club was also run by Pierce Coogan.

Doormen from the Assembly Club, 1960s. Left to right: the late Tom McGagh, Pierce Coogan, Tommy Coen, John Keane and Mick Kelly.

The Carousel,
Plymouth Grove,
Longsight, 1975.

A girls' night out at the Carousel, including Della Kilkenny, Mary Kilkenny, Tricia Galvin, Philomena Murphy and Bridie Galvin, 1970s.

The Welcome Inn, Rusholme Place/Hope Street, 1973.

The Farmhouse Kitchen, Wilmslow Road, Rusholme was owned by Kathleen Donnelly (the mother of the musician Dezi). Many Irish people enjoyed the welcome and the friendly atmosphere, which was just like home!

5

Radio & Media

The original team of *Irish Line*, 1985 (BBC Radio Manchester, Thursday 6.30–7.00pm).
Front row, left to right: Ian Murray (producer), Caroline Usher and Eamonn O'Neal.
Back row: Tony Farrell, Declan O'Neill, Peter Ledwith and Cllr Jim King (National Chairman of
the IBRG, in the studio to be interviewed). The playwright Eileen Murphy was not present but
had been involved throughout as a co-presenter of the programme.

Eamonn O'Neal writes:

In the early 1980s BBC Local Radio launched its Community Programmes initiative. In the North-West, BBC Radio Manchester, under the leadership of John McManus and his deputy, Steve Taylor, pioneered programmes made by and for the Afro-Caribbean, Chinese and Asian communities. It was the first time for many that their voices had been heard by a wider audience, and it was about time the Irish community got a piece of the action.

Credit must be given to the IBRG for its early work in lobbying for airtime. Michael Forde, Peter Ledwith and others persuaded the BBC that the Irish community could contribute from both a contemporary and a historical perspective. So was born *Irish Line* – a monthly programme produced and presented by a group of volunteers under the watchful eye of a BBC staff member. It wasn't all plain sailing. The political climate at that time meant it became increasingly difficult to find a mix of items that would satisfy everyone's objectives. Reluctantly, at the end of the run, the BBC decided not to recommission the programme.

However, as there was still an appetite for Irish culture, history and education on local radio, I was asked to gather a fresh team to produce a new programme. Together with Simon Greene, Alan Keegan, Tom McAndrew, Catherine McManus, Ged Hynes and Lawrence Graham, we consulted the many organisations, clubs and societies to gauge the level of interest from Manchester's first- and second-generation Irish people. With close cooperation and input from a wide cross section of interested parties, *Come into the Parlour* made it to air and was first broadcast in December 1985.

Come into the Parlour was unique on BBC radio and set the standard for those programmes on other radio stations across the country that were to follow. It enjoyed a success beyond our dreams. There were few Irish pubs that didn't play host to our outside broadcasts; there were few musicians who didn't get airplay and there were very few events that didn't get publicity. Each programme had imaginative and ground-breaking content. Live links with radio stations across Ireland and the USA, intercontinental celebrations for St Patrick's Day and a spectacular live concert with Daniel O'Donnell and Dezi Donnelly all remain wonderful memories. But the most important element of all has been the loyalty of the listeners.

After five years as presenter of *The Parlour*, I stepped aside to allow the programme to grow and develop. It was left in the more than capable hands of Alan, Simon and Ged and was augmented by the addition of Michael Kierans and others. Nineteen years on and *The Parlour* continues to serve the community. It is still staffed by volunteers (no one has ever been paid to work on the programme) and I'm immensely proud that members of that first team are there guiding it towards yet more milestones. Radio Manchester became BBC GMR and Alan Keegan has been presenting *The Parlour* for five years, supported by Simon Greene, Evelyn Grealy, Danny Murphy, Josephine Power, Bill Sweeney and many others. They're doing a marvellous job of 'keeping the faith' and their dedication should continue to be applauded.

In the early 1980s I had a vision. I was determined that Irish traditions and the work of the people should reach a wider and indigenous audience. Lots of people helped me realise that vision and the legacy lives on. I've since been in a position to continue the quest on television by commissioning a Granada TV series called *The Irish Connection*. We're still spreading the word.

The Parlour, rightly, has evolved over the years. Its style has changed and changed again but one thing remains constant – its commitment to celebrating Irish culture in the North-West. Broadcasting in the region is richer for it and we have a programme that continues to reach into the heart of who we are.

The new team of *Come into the Parlour*, 1985 (BBC Radio Manchester, every Wednesday, 7.00–8.00pm). Left to right: Simon Greene, Tom McAndrew, Michael Forde, Catherine McManus, Eamonn O'Neal and Alan Keegan.

How's the Craic (Sunset Radio) meets *The Parlour* (BBC GMR Talk Radio), 2 February 1991: Chris Duffy, Alan Keegan, Joe Casserley, Michael Kierans and Simon Greene. This photograph was taken at the Irish World Heritage Centre in the 1980s when both teams of 'rival' broadcasters turned up to interview the then Irish Minister of Labour, later to become the Taoiseach Bertie Ahern.

Mike Harding, seen here with many of the presenters and staff of Manchester Irish Radio, which was set up to go on 'Eire' in the summer of 1994. From left to right: Margaret Casserley, Rose Morris, Mike Harding, Marian Waldran, Eileen O'Boye, Tommie Casserley, Mark Kershaw, Angela Duffy, Stuart Smith, Maureen Burke, John Lowry, Catherine Thompson, Greg McNally, Trish Duffy, Anthony Walsh, John O'Brien and Ollie Mulloolley. It was the first of four Restricted Service Licences, that would broadcast twenty-four hours, for twenty-eight days, catering for all things Irish, even linking up with Paul Claffy for two hours every weekday on Mid-West Radio in County Mayo, providing the *Sound of Home* in Manchester. It broadcast at this time to coincide with the Republic of Ireland football team competing in the World Cup in America. The station was located on Mosley Road in Levenshulme, because after much research the census recorded that this was the most populated Irish area. After the success of the first two twenty-eight day, twenty-four hour broadcasts, the station gave its name to the Manchester Irish Festival, promoting the festival and providing a medium for publicity that it had never had before. It completed its last transmission from the committee meeting room in the Manchester Town Hall in March 1999. The commitment and dedication of all those who helped to make it a success will never be forgotten.

Opposite: How's the Craic, Sunset Radio 102FM, live on St Patrick's Day, 1991, from the Grove Club, Plymouth Grove, Longsight. Left to right: Paddy Johnson, Heather Ewing, Alan Keegan and Dave Lane. Broadcaster Mike Shaft achieved his dream on 22 October 1989 and set up the first full-time community radio station in Britain, and as part of his programming schedule he gave the Irish another voice and choice in Manchester. *How's the Craic* was born, presented by Alan Keegan and with a strong team that included Paddy Johnson (covering the GAA and Sport), Eileen O'Boye (the Irish language), Joe Casserley (interviews and entertainment guide), Dave Lane (association news), along with Philomena White, who was the voice on the phone taking the requests. (Many others contributed to the show, such as Chris Duffy, Trish and Sharon, Bridgit, Nuala, Dave and Lorraine.) The show was given a one-hour slot on a Friday night and the first guest was the popular Irish singer Dermot Hegarty. Because of its increasing popularity the programme was extended to four hours on a Sunday afternoon, reaching the heart and soul of the Irish community. It lasted for three years until the dream ended and Sunset Radio was taken off the air because of financial difficulties.

The third Manchester Irish Film Festival, 1990, organised by the IBRG in association with The Cornerhouse, Greater Manchester's arts and exhibition centre on Oxford Road. Left to right: Sandra Hebron, public relations officer for The Cornerhouse; Michael Herbert of the Manchester Irish History Group; Linda Sever, one of the organisers of the festival; and Phil Donnellan, who, with Seamus Ennis, made the acclaimed film *The Irishmen*, which was shown during the festival.

Michael Sheehan writes:

The Irish in Britain Representation Group was formed in 1981. Essentially it was a response to the hunger strikes of that year and the feeling that the Irish in Britain did not have an effective political organisation.

The *Irish Post* was crucial in establishing the IBRG. They published letters in the autumn of 1981 calling for the creation of a new organisation. The inaugural meeting of the new organisation was held in Newall, Burton-on-Trent in October 1981. Four people travelled across from Manchester: Rick Hennelly, Gerry Gallagher, Michael Sheehan and Patrick Sheehan.

The fledgling new group then began a series of rolling conferences in cities across Britain to establish new branches. The first meeting in Manchester was held at Our Lady's Parish Centre in Moss Side in December 1981. I recall that it was a bitterly cold day and a number of people could not get to the meeting because of the snow. Among those who attended the first meeting were Jim King, Michael Forde, Jimmy McGill, Harry McMurrough-Kavanagh, Donal O'Donoghue and Sean Sheahan. The stalwart of the Manchester Clare Association, Sean Hogan, was one of those who missed the meeting due to the weather conditions.

An agenda was set out at the meeting for the new group. This included: campaigning for justice in Ireland, defending the civil liberties of the Irish in Britain, challenging anti-Irish racism, providing access to the media, particularly local radio, including the Irish in multicultural approaches to education.

One of the early successes of Manchester IBRG was the broadcast of a programme on BBC2 entitled *The Irish: A Race Apart?* which was featured as part of the *Open Door* series. Early in 1982 the branch held its first social event at the Hunting Lodge on Oxford Road. There was music and entertainment over three floors of the club with St Wilfrid's Ceili band being particularly well received.

Over the years the branch was extremely active. In 1985 it established 'Irish Line', a weekly programme on BBC Radio Manchester. In 1984 it submitted a detailed report to Manchester City Council on the needs of the Irish in the city. When the council established a Race Committee made up of councillors and community representatives, two Irish representatives were elected. They were Ann Hilferty of the IBRG and Fr John Ahern, who at the time was the parish priest of St Lawrence's and Director of St Brendan's Irish Centre in City Road. One of the positive things to come out of IBRG's dialogue with the city council was a pledge that the authority would organise an annual Irish Week.

Many of IBRG's members were young second generation members of the community. Politically IBRG was significantly more radical than other Irish groups. Tension between IBRG and more conservative elements within the Irish community was therefore inevitable, however with hindsight it is fair to say that much of that tension was creative. The IBRG provided a catalyst for change and development. There is far less overt anti-Irish racism in the media than there was twenty years ago, which is in large measure because the IBRG made and won the argument that Irish people are entitled to the same respect as any other group in British society. In this city we have a weekly radio programme, an annual Irish week and an education group – all these are the products of seeds sown by the IBRG.

Over the past two decades Irish venues have been developed in the city and at one time virtually every county in Ireland was represented by an association in Manchester. There has also been a huge growth in Irish awareness among second and third generation Irish in the city. The IBRG contributed greatly to this revival of things Irish in our city.

The Second Generation. Joe Casserley, Mike Cunningham, Greg McNally, Ollie Mulloolley and Alan Keegan, all DJs in the Irish community, late 1980s.

Opposite, top: Tommy Golden, the proprietor of the *Irish Gazette*, seen here with TV and radio broadcaster Eamonn O'Neal, 1995.

Opposite: A Gaelic class at Ducie High School, 1985. Lessons were given by Lena Daly, standing on the extreme left.

The Manchester Irish Education Group, 1992. Standing, left to right: Walter Cassin, Les Hankin, Karen Bates, Pat Hoswell and Seamus Morgan. Seated: Joe Flynn and Janet Wallwork.

Joe Flynn writes:

The Manchester Irish Education Group was founded in 1986. Our aim is to promote a positive image of Ireland and the Irish in schools, community, colleges and universities. We believe that the large Irish community should have access to its cultural background and that this should be shared with others. But more than this we try to give support to people of any age who want to explore and reaffirm their Irish identity.

Achievements:

Annual Irish Studies classes

Irish language classes for adults and for children

Irish cultural studies in schools

School trips to Ireland

Negotiated and lobbied for more Irish language books in public libraries

Literature and art competitions for children

Survey of the Irish community on the education of their children and presentation of findings to ten local authorities in the region

National Irish Studies Award

Irish Heritage Magazine

Trips to places of interest and to conferences

Irish Post Award for Community service.

6

Dance Bands &
Entertainment

Des Byrne and the Skyliners, seen here at the Sharrocks Irish Club, 1953.

Richard Walsh and his Blarney Boys at the Blond Hall, 1950s. Left to right: Sean Wheellan, Mick Breen, Richard Walsh, Seamus O'Rourke and Jimmy Riley.

The Banba Blarney Band, 1950s. Included here are Jim Dunlea (third from the left), Jimmy Byrne (at the microphone), Paddy Feery (on sax) and Jim Dunlea Jr (wearing glasses).

Margaret and Tommie Casserley. Margaret McGloughlin the singer met Tommie Casserley the musician in 1959. In April 1960 they were married and moved to Birmingham from Ireland. Five years later they moved to Manchester and settled in the Chorlton area.

Below: The Wild Rovers Band, 1969. Oliver Claffey senior on accordion, Paddy Donnelly on banjo, Oli Claffey on banjo and Danny Claffey (the same Danny Claffey that is the photographer) on drums.

The Ranchers Showband, 1972. Left to right: Ned Brennan, Pat Jordan, Mike Brennan, John Keenan and Jimmy Brennan.

Mike Brennan writes:

The Ranchers Showband was formed in 1968. The original members were the brothers Mike, Ned and Jim Brennan, along with Pat Jordan and John Keenan. Pat Jordan was with the Ranchers for seven years before he went on to join the Carousel Band and was replaced by the singer Dusty, who was with the band for about eight years. John Keenan was with the band for fifteen years before he left to open the 32 Club, which was previously St Aloysius in Ardwick Green.

Another popular member of the band was Kevin Fox, who was with them for ten years, only leaving for health reasons. Other members over the years have included Christy Burn, Mark and Eddie Byrne, Johnny Peters, Bob King, Tony Sullivan, Brian Howard, Mary O'Brien, Ash and Paul Pickering. The line up as I write is still the Brennan brothers, Mike, Ned and Jim along with Ned's son Darren and Brendan Forkan.

Part and parcel of the local music scene, Tony Howley is one of the real gentlemen of Irish traditional music.

Below: The Downbeats. Paddy McNally on guitar, Tommy McGuire on guitar, Peter Holland on drums and Mike Cosgrove on keyboard. Pete Holland is from County Leitrim. He has been involved in the Irish music scene since the mid-1960s with residencies in the Lancaster on Stockport Road in Longsight, the Ram on Oldham Road, and the Irish Association Club in Chorlton. The band then decided to go on the road and had a change of name, becoming Country Breeze.

The Sweeney Brothers and Kevin Fox. Left to right: Eddie Sweeney, Padraig Sweeney, Kevin Fox and Sean Sweeney. This is one of the many bands that entertained the Irish community over the years with their brand of country and Irish music. Known as Livestock for many years, they were the resident band in St Mary's parish centre, Levenshulme.

THE SWEENEY BROTHERS
AND KEVIN FOX

Aidan and the Strangers (Mike O'Brien, Duncan Mulvey and Hughie Cummins on drums) on stage at St Brendan's.

Kevin Prendergast writes:

I came to Manchester in or around 1963 and started work as a barman in a pub on Oxford Road. I also worked on building sites driving pick-up trucks for some of the Irish contractors. At weekends I would visit the Irish clubs and pubs and give a few songs. In 1981 I made my first record, a song I composed entitled 'Let's go back to County Mayo'. Being a Ballyhaunis man I thought it appropriate to write one for my own county. Since then I have released several tapes and CDs and one video. I spend most of my time touring throughout Ireland but always come back to Manchester, where I have many friends. I would like to thank the people of Manchester and indeed throughout Britain who have put me where I am today.

Paddy and the Wild Country. Back row, left to right: Johnny Buckley, Denis Tongue and Jim Burns. Front row: Nick Stone and Paddy McElherron.

The Countrysiders, early 1980s. Standing: Brian Robb and Johnny Loughrey. Kneeling: Timmy Bergin and Paul Lacey.

Steve Flynn, Chris Reilly, Pat Jordan, Kieran Towey and Tony Corrigan – Finian's Rainbow. This was one of the most popular bands on the Manchester Irish music scene. Pat Jordan began his musical career with another Irish band in Manchester, the Ranchers.

The Borderline Showband was formed in 1983. This was the sleeve for their cassette *People Like You*. Left to right: Jimmy Prendergast (lead guitar, rhythm guitar, lead and backing vocals), Peter Corbett (drums), Brendan Forkan (lead and backing vocals), Ged Graham (lead and backing vocals, rhythm guitar, bass guitar) and Dave Meagh (keyboards, strings and accordion). Other members have included Kevin Kennedy and Geraldine Howley.

Brendan & Ramblin' Feelin'. Brendan Forkan presents the Amy Fleming Award, given to a special person in the Irish community on an annual basis. Frank Fleming is far left. The band were Duncan Mulvey, Brendan Forkan, Eddie Byrne, Gareth Walsh and Johnny Buckley.

The Dublin Rogues. Left to right: Billy Barton, Owen John, Dave Thom, Mike McNally and John Barton. The Barton brothers were famous for their songs and stories.

Joe Kennedy conducting the Kennedy Swinton Brass Band (British Open Champions). The Kennedy Swinton Band is part of a long distinguished history of brass bands, which have existed in one form or another in the north Manchester town of Swinton since 1876. The band has won many competitions, both here and in Australia and made a number of BBC radio broadcasts, making it one of the country's most successful and popular brass bands.

Brian Breen (fourth from left, sitting with accordion) and friends, late 1970s.

Vinny Donnelly with his cousin
Dezi Donnelly.

St Wilfrid's junior band, 1977.
Andrew Dinan is on banjo. Among the
group are Eileen Egan, Elizabeth Egan
and Marie Egan.

Paul Farrell and Kevin Deasy,
with Gino Lupari and
Lawrence Hennigan at the
Palace nightclub, St Patrick's
Day, 1996.

Above: Toss the Feathers, without doubt one of the most popular Celtic rock bands to come out of Manchester, early 1980s. Back row, left to right: Dezi Donnelly, Dave Smylie. Middle row: Eddie Sheehan, Mike McGoldrick, Angela Usher. Front row: Peter Carberry, Paul Usher. *Right:* Skidoo, 1990s. *Below:* Ceile, 1990s.

6

Dancers, Processions & Parades

Kerry Pipers during the Whit Walk in Manchester at the junction of Piccadilly and
Portland Street (Lever Street is in the background), 1953.

Major influences in the Irish music and dance scene. From left to right: Norah Lynott, Betty Kelly and Norah Walsh, 1973.

Norah Walsh (née Lynott) writes:

My mother, Norah Lynott (née Keane), came from a little place called Ballyashee, outside Ennis, County Clare. She emigrated to England in 1919 at the age of thirteen. She met and married my father (he emigrated to England from Laken, outside Ballina, County Mayo) in the 1920s. They had ten children: Rita, Norah, Sheila, Margaret, Ann, Martin, Pat, Susan, John and Mary. My father played the melodeon and my mother loved Irish dancing and she wanted her children to learn to play music and to dance. Mother made enquiries and found out there was a Betty Kelly who was teaching a little girl at her home in Slater Street, Collyhurst. The little girl was Kathleen Walsh. I later married her brother, Richard.

Betty Kelly first came into our lives in the early 1940s when she used to come to our home with her violin and teach us to dance. At the time she lived in Stock Street, Cheetham Hill, in the parish of St Chad's, where the young curate, the Revd Fr Garry, arranged for her to use the school to teach dancing. He watched over us all and encouraged us in all things Irish. He himself was an excellent singer. Fr Garry also organised dances, which were held in the school hall every Saturday and Sunday night. Betty played the violin and her brother Kevin played the accordion. Seamus O'Rourke played the drums and Maggie Richardson played the piano. There was no drink involved except a cup of tea and a piece of cake. They were most enjoyable evenings of good fun. Even when Betty had left the area, she still used the name St Chad's for her dancers. Betty first taught us the baby reel, light jig, hornpipe, blackbird, four-hand reel, Humours of Bandon, High-Cauled Cap, sixteen-hand reel and many ceili dances. She then engaged dancers from Ireland to teach us more advanced steps and entered us in many competitions. I passed my teacher's exam, as did many of Betty's pupils, and taught step dancing and ceili dancing in the late 1950s and 1960s. In 1980 Sean Dempsey asked me if I would teach a group of people to ceili dance. I did this for a number of years and then we became involved with the old style of set dancing.

Not only did Betty teach us to dance and play music; she also made our uniforms. At first we, in our family, all had different coloured kilts and blouses, then she decided on a class costume, which consisted of a green pleated skirt, a white blouse and a gold broth. We used to wear the patent leather hornpipe shoes with the silver buckles. At a later date the black velvet bolero was added to the uniform and later still Mrs Grainger made beautiful satin blouses with big colours and this was the completed uniform. The only embroidery to be seen was on the broths and we did wear tara brooches to keep them in place.

Betty had a wonderful way with people. She had a great sense of humour (sometimes even wicked). Not only did she teach us to step dance and ceili dance; she taught us to sing, recite poetry and play music. Betty organised Ceilis and fund-raising functions as far back as the 1940s. She organised a junior Ceili Band (mostly made up of Lynotts): Sheila on the piano, Rita and Norah on fiddles and an Italian boy (I think his name was Carlo Giovanni) on drums. She also organised the first ever Manchester Feish. In these early competitions there would be step dancing, figure dancing, singing, fiddle competitions and piano competitions. Betty took her dancers to competitions the length and breadth of England and in 1948 she was the first teacher to take step dancers to the Fr Matthew Feis in Dublin. Later she took her dancers to Newry. It wasn't all dancing though; she managed to arrange for trips to the seaside, climbing Bray Head. She took us to Trinity College in Dublin to see the Book of Kells and to Matt Talbot's grave in Glasnevin cemetery. Betty was full of life and had a very generous nature.

St Chad's Dancers, photographed at St Malachy's School, Collyhurst, near Rochdale Road, 1944.

The Gaelic League dancers, taught by Margaret O'Neal, seen here at the Free Trade Hall, 1950s. Eileen Lally, May Connolly, Anne Kelly (Mrs Callaghan), Anne Kennedy, Anne Callaghan (Frank's sister), Maureen Smith, Eileen and Geraldine Smith, Maureen Ward, Winifred Watson, Eileen Smith, Ann and Bernadette Moore, Barbara Aherne (née Doyle), Carol Egan, Patricia Burke, Rosemary Lally, Patricia Lally, Michael Lally, Maureen Lee, Ann Hagan, Paul Callaghan (Frank's younger brother), Angela Egan, Sean Earley and Agnes Earley,

The MacSwiney Pipe Band, St Patrick's Day, 1946.

Kathleen Houldsworth writes:

The MacSwiney Pipe Band was started in 1920 in Manchester. It was the first one here. It was Father O'Sullivan from Ballyduff, a curate at St Patrick's, who started it. The Dermody family took over from him. All the Dermody boys, Dennis, Phil, Chris and Anthony, were in the band.

Kathleen Houldsworth and Annie Walsh.

Fianna Padraig Pipe Band and Dancers of St John's, Benchill, Wythenshawe at the International Eisteddfod at Llangollen, North Wales, 1951. Back row, left to right: Jimmy Clark, Margaret O'Neal (née Carroll), Des Keenan, Michael Barker, Fr Kehoe and Brian Lee. Middle row: Collette Richardson, Steve Brennan, Peter Fitzpatrick, Terry Forde and May Connolly. Front row: Joan Maguire, Clare Roache, Betty Hussey and Josie Coady.

St Joseph's Drum and Fife Band, Salford, 1955. They trained on Tib Street near the B & I office.

St Sebastian's Pipe Band, Broad Street, Salford, 1962. The band is being led by Sammy Locke; also included are Patrick McKenna, Wally Pegg, Terry Graham and John Vause.

St Sebastian's Pipe Band on a Trinity Sunday Walk, passing St Sebastian's Church, Gerald Road, Salford. Among those seen here are Sammy Locke, Terry Graham, Mike Duff, Wally Pegg, Tom Martin, Patrick McKenna and John Martin,

The dance team of Lamhdheirg. Some of the dancers seen here are Ann Cunningham, Oliver McNulty, Rose Fitzgibbon, Sean Callaghan and Mary Hefferan.

The Margaret O'Neal School of Dancing, taking part in the Wythenshawe Procession, St Anthony's, 1969. The young boy at the front is John Morgan; also seen here are Bernadette O'Neal, Ann McKelvey, Bernadette Heaney, Patricia Heaney, Geraldine Heaney, Bernadette Hennessy and Geraldine O'Neal.

Dancers at Chorlton-cum-Hardy Town Hall, 1950s. Left to right: Dinah Duffy, Brenda Grainger, Norah Lynott, Joan Hyland and Kathleen Kelly.

The Irish World Heritage Centre Pipe Band, led by Frank Judge and Trish Brady, late 1980s.

Frank Judge writes:

I started the band in 1986. We only had three or four members with no funds or uniforms. I was elected chairman/treasurer and was later joined by Vincent and Trish Brady. Vincent became the secretary and Trish joined us as an experienced piper which was what we needed. To raise funds I ran the Manchester Piccadilly Marathon (in a kilt) – the £300 helped to buy a full set of second-hand uniforms in Dublin.

Musicians in 1948. Left to right: Eileen Lally, Mary Abbott, Theresa Roca, Norah Lynott, Margaret Roca, Mary Dillon and Joan Hyland.

Terry Dowling receives the Mayo Annual Award on behalf of the Fianna Padraig Pipe Band from Marcella Wilkinson at the Lancashire County Cricket Club, 1988.

The Grainger School of Dancing, seen here with the Rose of Tralee, 1987. The dancers seen here include Sinead O'Donnell, Suzanne Weldon, Tracy Costello, Michelle Knight, Catrina Mooney, Joseph Lynch, Martina Lyons, Geraldine Lyons, Mary Farrell and Paula Costello.

YGG celebrating the Manchester Irish Festival with the actor Kevin Kennedy and the owner of the Palace nightclub, Lawrence Hennigan, 1996.

Barbara Aherne writes:

Sean Dempsey dancing with Rose Morris.

Sean Dempsey was born in Wexford and came to Manchester at about eight years of age. He was brought up in Manchester. He was quite taken by the ceili dancing when he first saw it being done. He decided to get a group together and I believe it was his father who told him that he would have to start by getting himself a dancing teacher. Norah Walsh was the dancing teacher recommended to him and a class was started in St Dunstan's, eventually moving into St Malachy's hall under the school. Here the children were taught music, and the ceili class followed on afterwards. I had heard a lot about the ceili club, but it clashed with the night we attended dancing at the Chorlton club, where my children and I went for lessons with Margaret O'Neal.

Margaret O'Neal retired from dancing in the 1980s and at first I kept going to the classes at Chorlton, which were then conducted by Caroline Usher, under the title of Lally School. Then her sister Angela started a class at the Irish World Heritage Centre, which was much nearer so we decided to go there. Then I changed Bridget to Morgan School and as soon as the St Malachy's ceili club and music group moved into the centre I was able to join them for the classes on a Monday night. I had done some set dancing with Margaret O'Neal in previous years. The first set dance workshops in the Irish World Heritage Centre were actually organised by the McDaid family, who were all studying at Manchester University, and some of whom are excellent musicians.

Sean came up with the idea of having the Manchester International Set Dance Festival. The first festival took place at the Irish World Heritage Centre in October 1988. The weather was absolutely lovely and the festival was a great success. We had the marquee in the car park, great competitions and great ceili each night. At that time we also had people doing workshops for part of the day. In 1989 we had our second festival at the Irish World Heritage Centre, but because of the dreadful weather it was almost a disaster. The dressing tent blew over the fencing at the side near the bus terminal, the marquee was awash with the rain and it was dreadfully cold. That was when Sean decided to look for a new venue.

In 1990 we moved to the Forum at Wythenshawe. In the first years the workshops, competitions and ceili were all well attended, but in subsequent years the workshops eventually dropped off, so we decided just to carry on with competitions and ceili.

Sean really put Manchester on the map for set dancing.

The Manchester Irish
Festival banner displayed
with pride at the front of
the Manchester Town Hall,
2003.

President Mary Robinson is welcomed to the Manchester Irish Festival by the Mayor of Manchester, Derek Shaw,
and his wife, Sue, along with the chair of the Irish Festival Committee, Councillor Pat Karney, June 1996.

Mary McAleese (soon to be President) is welcomed to the Irish World Heritage Centre by the chairman Michael Forde, 1997.

Peter (the Great) Merrigan is surprised with a special version of *This Is Your Life*, held at the English Martyrs' parish centre, June 1997, to show appreciation of his hard work for the Irish Community and in particular for the Council of Irish Associations, of which he was chairman from 1994 until his untimely death in 1997. Left to right: Tim Joyce, Bernadette Merrigan, Peter Merrigan, Paddy Geoghegan, Tom and Maureen McGoff.

The Armagh
Association at
the Manchester
Irish Festival
Parade, 2003,
led by Maria
Sowerby and
Sinead
Sweeney.

Rose Morris on the Tyrone Association parade float, 2001. The association was founded in April 1987.

The Galway Association was founded on 28 January 1981. Forty-eight people attended the first meeting, addressed by Pat Sweeney, which was held at Our Lady's Social Club. The first committee comprised Tadgh Meehan (president), Gerry O'Reilly (chairman), Pascal Madden (vice chairman), Rita Mitchell (secretary), Sean Clarke (assistant secretary) and John Divanney (treasurer). The first fund-raising dance was held at Our Lady's Social Club in May 1981, and the first dinner dance at the Manor Hey Hotel, Urmston, May 1982.

The Roscommon Association was founded in 1987, the first dance being at St Brendan's, Old Trafford. This gathering was in 1993. Back row, left to right: Frank Fox, Austin Smith, Chris Mannion, Eugene McDonagh, Dave Lane and John Carney. Front row: Gertie Mannion, Ann Carney, Maureen Fox, Pat Smith, Masie Docherty and Margaret Casserley.

The first Cavan Association dance was held on 29 April, 1983. This group are celebrating the launch of the Manchester Irish Festival at Manchester Town Hall, March 1999. Left to right: Liam Goldrick, Kath McGrath, Gerry McGrath, Marcella McEntee, Ray Tully, Tony Lloyd MP, Eugene McEntee and Margaret Goldrick.

Liam McGloughlin and Paddy Hynes, representing Conradh Na Gaeilge (the Gaelic League) in the Manchester Irish Festival Parade.

The Leitrim Association was founded in 1982. Its committee members and friends are seen here enjoying a dinner dance at the Manor Hey Hotel, Urmston.

Sam Murray driving one of his vintage cars in the parade.

The Louth Association was founded in 1995. Some people thought that a Manchester County Louth Association had been formed in the late 1950s or early 1960s following the emigration of large numbers from Ireland to Manchester during the 1940s and 1950s. However, in 1995 nobody from the Louth area knew of it, so on 19 September 1995 the Association was born, or reborn. A meeting was held in Biddy Mulligan's pub on Stockport Road, Longsight, and was attended by fifteen people in response to a notice in the *Irish Post* by John Martin. Those in attendance were Tommy Cunningham, Frank and Bridgit Elmore, Mary Gray, Phil Gray, John Martin, Paddy and Kitty Healy, Betty Fahy, Phil and Mona Walsh, Benny Woods, Jimmy O'Hanlon, Susan Smith and Paddy Moore.

The Carlow Association, 2003. The association was established in 1991.

The Armagh Association was founded in 1998 in response to a radio appeal by Mr John Martin.

The Kilkenny Association was originally formed by a group of Kilkenny supporters returning to Manchester after watching the 1978 All Ireland Hurling Final. A meeting was held at the Holy Name Social Club, All Saints, to elect a committee, and the first fund-raising dance was held at the Holy Name Social Club on 6 January 1978. The first dinner dance was held at the Lancashire County Cricket Club in 1979. The editor of the *Kilkenny People*, John Kerry Keane, Senator Michael Lanagan and Hurler Eddie Keher were among the guests. Jim O'Shea was the first president, Jim Phelan the first chairman and the late Jim Gordon the first secretary. The association has had a number of presidents, chairmen and treasurers over the years, but only two ladies have taken the role of secretary, Mrs Rosie Hynes and the present secretary, Mrs Maureen Aylward, who has been a guiding force behind the association for many years.

Members of the Dublin Association, which was founded on 15 January 1987.

Sean Herron, Michael Murphy, Pat O'Keefe and Paddy Moore of the Tipperary Association.

The Mayo Association of Manchester was inaugurated in 1980 and held its first annual dinner dance in February 1981. The first elected committee consisted of Tony Deasey (Bohola) as president, Tom McAndrew (Bangor Ennis) as chairperson, Michael Forde (Kiltamagh) as secretary and the late Jimmy Henelly (Ballindine) as treasurer. Here we see members of the Mayo Association boarding the plane at Manchester Airport to attend Mayo's first convention in Westport, 1990. From the top: Jim Prendergast, Eileen Hester, Tom Duffy, Mary Regan, Peter Walsh and Pat McCormack.

7

The Gaelic Athletic Association & Sport

Paddy Johnson and friends of the Oisin GAA, 1998.

The GAA in Lancashire

In 1963, Chairman T. Walsh wrote in the programme notes: 'Today, we write a page of history – we play a Junior All-Ireland Final, here in Manchester.'

The first games recorded in Lancashire took place in Greenwich Park, Aintree, Liverpool, in 1905. Little is known of the details of the competitions of this period and although it is known that hurling and gaelic football were played at the same venue for many years, it was not until 1926 that the affairs of the association became really well organised. Central Council sent over to Britain a Mr McGrath and he reorganised and revitalised the GAA in the whole of this country. As a result, the Provincial Council of Britain was formed in 1926. At that time it consisted of Liverpool and District County Board (as Lancashire was then known) and London. These two counties between them fielded the British team which met Meath, All-Ireland Junior Hurling Champions, at Dundalk in 1927, going down by two points after a hard-fought game.

In 1929 the first team to represent Lancashire at hurling (being selected from Liverpool and Manchester) met Cork in Croke Park and went down by a few points.

In more recent times our successes have been at football. We have won the Provincial Championship of Britain four times in the last fourteen years. In 1949 we met Kerry in Croke Park; in 1953 Cork at the Athletic Grounds, Cork; and we travelled to Ballinasloe to meet Galway in 1958. All these games were lost by a few points.

The Lancashire GAA, 1998.

The Lancashire County Board GAA, 1940. Seated, left to right: J. Ryan (vice-chairman), Revd Spain (chairman and hurling captain), J. McInerney (treasurer). Standing: G. Mulholland (secretary and football captain), P. O'Neill (assistant secretary).

REG. HARRIS (MANCHESTER) LTD.

HARRIS STADIUM, FALLOWFIELD, MANCHESTER, 14

Directors
R. H. HARRIS
D. HARRIS

Telephone
RUSholme 1378

NG/MH.   January 9th.1959.

H.J.Purcell,Esq.,
Waverley Hotel,
Grafton Street,
MANCHESTER 13.

Dear Mr.Purcell,

        Thank you for your recent letter confirming to
terms of hire for the Stadium by your Association.

        We are in agreement that your opening game will
take place on Sunday, February 15th.

        With regards to the Double Fixture date, I suggest
we leave this until later to see what Sunday morning
football we have booked.

        I have just written to Frank Flynn telling him that
we can purchase steel goal posts,if you wish,at the
following prices:-

        Black   —   £14.19.0.

        Galvanised White —   £15.10.0.

        Wishing you a most successful season,

                        Kind regards,

                        Yours sincerely,

                        Reg Harris(Manchester)Ltd.
                            General Manager.

Letter to Harry Purcell from the Harris Stadium, Fallowfield, regarding the hire of the facilities, 1959.

CUMANN LUITH-CHLEAS CAEDHEAL
GAELIC ATHLETIC ASSOCIATION

MICHAEL CUSACK
Founder of the Association
ALL-IRELAND JUNIOR FOOTBALL CHAMPIONSHIP
FINAL
LANCASHIRE v KERRY
WHITE CITY STADIUM
MANCHESTER
at 3-30 p.m.
SUNDAY, 6th OCTOBER, 1963
also at 2 p.m. Lancs. Hurling Championship Final
HARP AND SHAMROCK v. MOINDEARG
Cead Mile Failte

All-Ireland Junior Final programme, Lancashire v Kerry, 1963.

THE LANCASHIRE FOOTBALL PANEL WHICH WON THE 1977 PROVINCIAL CHAMPIONSHIP OF
BRITAIN AND WERE N.F.L. DIVISION 2 RUNNERS-UP

The Lancashire Football Panel that won the 1977 Provincial Championship of Great Britain and were NFL Division 2 runners-up.

The St Brendan's Irish Club, 1992. Patsy Connolly from Monaghan, Pat Scally from Offaly and Dermot Redmond from Dublin with the Sam McGuire Cup.

GAA President Peter Quinn visits Lancashire. Back row, left to right: Joe Cahill, Paddy Johnson, Pat Farry, Michael Connors. Front row: Fr John Ahern, Peter Quinn, Barney Keable.

Oisin under-14 Champions of Britain, 1984.

B & I presentation with Margaret Curry and friends, including Harry Purcell, Paddy Johnson, Michael Butler and Tadgh Meehan.

St Peter's GAA football team, 1988.

St Peter's and Sarsfield Gaels hurling team, 1990.

St Kentigern's GAA Junior Championship side, 1993. Back row, left to right: Anthony Morin, Gabriel Dowd, Jimmy O'Leary, John Grealy (manager), Dessie Donnelly, Joe Cunningham, Tom Egan, Pat Scally, John Maloney, Dermot Scally. Front row: Jimmy Lambe, Jim Conama, Patsy Connolly, Kevin O'Gara, Kevin McCormack, Brian Noone, Philip Hester, Steve Kenny, Ged Noonan; Children: Niall Connolly, Liam Connolly, Claire Connolly, Ashley Dowd, Kieran Dowd, Jennifer Noone, Paul Noone, Sinead Dowd.

St Lawrence's GAA Club committee at the then Valley Lodge Hotel, Wilmslow, Cheshire. Back row, left to right: Eddie Lyons, Tom Duffy, Frank Keane, Kieran Meally, Jim O'Shea, Tom Brehan, Tim Breen, Mikey Sheehey, Noel Burke, the late Harry Purcell. Front row: Paddy Johnson, John Dowling, Kevin Fullen, Fr John Ahern, the late Michael Butler.

St Brendan's under-10s, 1996.

Lancashire Ladies, 1998.

Delegates at the Lancashire GAA
Convention on the steps of the Irish
Association Club in Chorlton, 1998.

Lancashire GAA, 1998.

Oisin under-14s, 1998.

St Lawrence's Lancashire Junior Champions, 1998.

St Lawrence's Lancashire Senior Champions, 1998.

St Lawrence's GAA, 1992/3.

GAA Committee and members. Back row, left to right: John Reilly, Eddie Hogan, John Connors, Michael Connors, Andy O'Dwyre, Eamon Finnerty, John Joe Toland, Declan O'Boyle. Front row: Eamon Cahill, Peter King, Tommy Brennan, Peter Connors, Seamus Connors, Sean McGirl, Jim Brett.

8

Celebrities &
Special Events

The Irish Association Club, Chorlton, 1968. Sir Matt Busby (centre) shows the European Cup, which Manchester United had won that year, to Cath and Tom Connors.

Angela Greene writes:

At the end of the 1940s many Irish graduates found it difficult to get jobs in Ireland. At the same time England desperately needed doctors, nurses, teachers, engineers and accountants, and so started a big emigration wave of Irish professional and business people. To cater for these young men and women, a group calling itself the Wild Geese Club was founded in 1956. It started off in a modest way from a pub in Chorlton called the Royal Oak, where Jim Quinn, Niall McCormack, Malachy Glynn, Nancy Moriarty, Paddy Keely, Alec Eaton, Tom Glennon and Angela McCormack met to organise a gathering of Irish emigrants looking for the fellowship of their countrymen.

It was decided that it should be a 32-county club, where people of both cultures, North and South, would be welcome. This was an unusual feature in those days, when North and South seldom met socially or culturally. It grew very quickly, news of it spreading entirely by word of mouth until it became clear that acquisition of premises of its own was imperative. These premises were eventually found on Palatine Road in Didsbury. Very soon dinner dances and concerts of Irish artistes such as Maire Ni Scolaidhe, Brendan O'Dowda and Michael O'Higgins were organised and enjoyed by the members. A big event every year was the St Patrick's Day dinner dance, held in one of Manchester's leading hotels of the era.

Another very popular club activity founded by Teresa Gilbride was a dramatic society, where many Sean O'Casey plays were performed, sometimes with hilarious results! Who remembers John Kelly's performance in *Juno and the Paycock?*

The club began to decline in the late 1960s when many members returned to Ireland to pursue their careers. Others married here and found that club life did not fit in with their new responsibilities. At this time emigration of Irish professionals dried up as Ireland began to organise institutions and needed its own trained personnel.

But even forty years on, whenever members meet they still enjoy reminiscing over the enjoyable times they spent in the Wild Geese Club of Manchester.

The Wild Geese at the Grand Hotel, 1959. Gertie and Des O'Hora with Ted and Una Charleson and Frank and Angela Greene.

Winning darts team celebration at the Lancaster Pub, Stockport Road, Longsight, 1970s. Those in the photo include Eda O'Neary (landlady), Tom Coney, Peter O'Neary (landlord), Peter Quinn, Johnny Maher, Tommy Duffy, Madge Duffy, Jim Short, Vincent McCarten, Mrs Nelly Maher, Margaret Coney, Mannion, Mary Davenport and Dotie Keegan.

Ray Tully writes:

I was born in Cavan town in Ulster from a long line of Labour Party members dating back to my grandfather. I have been happy and proud to be able to serve the Manchester Irish. I still am. All good wishes.

The Mayor of Trafford, 1992–3. Councillor Ray Tully has come a long way from Cavan town in Ulster.

John Joe Lally and Joe Dunphy with family and friends at the Irish Association Club, Chorlton.

HRH Queen Elizabeth the Queen Mother presenting the Tote Cheltenham Gold Cup to Tim and Loretta Kilroe, on the occasion of their horse, Forgive 'n' Forget, winning the race, 1985.

Mr and Mrs Joe and Kathleen Kennedy being conferred with the Knighthood of St Gregory the Great by Pope John Paul II, 2002. He is now known as Sir Joe and his wife is Lady Kathleen. Daughter Cathy is observing.

The official opening of Francis House in Didsbury, where the 'Golden Girls' were introduced to Princess Diana, 25 November 1991. Those present include Mary Curley, Vera Thornhill, Jean McGrath, Pat Morgan and Eileen Lonergan. The 'unofficial' photographer at the back is Archie Thornhill.

Dusty Young first came to Manchester in the 1960s as a musician with the Kings Showband from Naas, County Kildare, and played in the Sharrocks Ballroom and the Astoria. He is pictured here at the Piccadilly Hotel with the BBC commentator, Kenneth Wolstenholme, Sir Alex Ferguson, the Manchester United manager, and Nat Basso, the famous boxing promoter, 1991.

Kilroe tug-of-war team, champions of the world, 1985. The all-Irish Kilroe tug-of-war team, based in Manchester, went to Chicago and came back world champions. To get to Chicago, the team had to win through in Britain, including taking the all-Britain title. The winning team comprised; Sean, Kevin, Paddy, Michael and Aidan Reilly (with a sixth brother, Billy, as coach), as well as Tommy Burke and Tommy Rowland. The team are seen here with Tommy Galvin of Aran Travel and the proprietor of the New Ardri, Tom McKenna.

John Hulme and friends, 17 March 1987. Left to right: John Hulme, Paddy Curley, Chris Kennedy, Joseph Kennedy, Joe Kennedy, Edward Kennedy and Harold Riley.

A night out at the Ardri, late 1960s. Back row, left to right: Ursula Fallon, Madge Keegan, Ena Rafferty, Dotie Keegan, Bernie Rafferty, Mary Deignan, Margaret Tiernan and Florence Fallon. Front row: Peter Holland, Maura Rafferty, Beatrice Roache and Aidan Kennedy.

Councillor John Commons from County Mayo chats with broadcaster Terry Christian at the Manchester Irish Festival launch in the Town Hall.

A sporting get-together, 1988. Left to right: Paddy McGrath, George Best, Sir Matt Busby, Paddy Curley and Johnny Carey.

Christy O'Connor and John O'Leary give Joe Kennedy a few golfing tips, 1972.

President Mary Robinson visits Irish Community Care, 289 Cheetham Hill Road, in 1994. This project came from an original idea and dream of Fr Emmet Fullen and was developed by Fr John Ahern, Michael Forde, Tom McKenna, Jim Coll and Pat Sweeney, along with many volunteers from the Irish community.

The Lord Mayor's Emergency Appeal Fund, 1996. Left to right: Susan and Derek Shaw with Tony and Maggie Hennigan.

After completing his charity run, Mike Coen presents broadcaster Suzie Mathis with a cheque for the Kirsty Howard Appeal for Francis House, 2003.

Above: World champion Irish Dancer James Keegan. *Left:* Louise and James Keegan. Louise shows the World Champion a few steps.

ACKNOWLEDGEMENTS

The pleasure of collecting these photographs has been a real labour of love. A special thanks to Danny Claffey for his support and enthusiasm; also to Anne (the Leitrim Light) Bohan Taghian; to the many friends, old and new, who made the research and visits extremely enjoyable, and supplied endless cups of tea; to my family for their love, support and patience. Please continue to send me more photographs and memories, as the story of the Irish in Manchester is never-ending: Irish Manchester, PO Box 40, Manchester, M19 2HN, or visit the website: www.irishmanchester.com.

The following helped me in various ways or lent, and gave me permission to reproduce, photographs: D. Claffey, P. McKenna, the Fahey family, Irish Community Care, M. Forde, T. McKenna, Francis Beirne, P. Sweeney, M. Sweeney, D. Murphy, P. Curley, J.P. Kennedy, A. Murphy, M. Logan, P. McGuinness, G. Noonan, P. Keegan, D. Costello, P. Costello, J. Kennedy, M. O'Brien, M. Butler, T. Galvin, J. Phelan, M. Fitzgerald, M. Lally, T. Finnigan, M. Curry, C. McDonald, T. Hennigan, L. Hennigan, D. Hennigan, M. Nash, the Coogan family, T. McGoff, S. Fisher, C. Breen, S. Keegan, H. Keegan, J. Loughrey, M. Cagney, M. Sheehan, K. Donnelly, M. Keegan, M. Burke, P. Rafter, D. Young, the Griffin family, M. Casserley, J. Casserley, J. Wrynne, P. Moore, R. Morris, N. Walsh, M. Byrne, M. Brennan, C. Connor, T. Howley, P. Holland, K. Prendergast, P. Jordan, D. Mulvey, J. Flynn, W. Cassin, B. Aherne, W.P. Fitzpatrick, C. Duffy, M. O'Neal, F. Judge, T. Duffy, V. Gillett, M. Connors, B. Attree, P. Farry, J. McGuinness, A. Greene, J. Commons, R. Tully, P. Kilroe, M. Coen, M. Dundon, Fr J. Ahern, S. Healey, E. O'Neal, L. McGloughlin, Betty Donelon, V. Kennedy, R. Bohan, Ian Penney, Anne Bohan Taghian, J. Keegan. Friends and colleagues at the University of Central Lancashire, especially Tony Clancy; the brilliant team that work at BBC GMR (*The Parlour*). Thanks also to Simon Fletcher, Hilary Walford and Michelle Tilling at Sutton Publishing.

My sincere thanks to each and every one, and my apologies for any omissions or errors which may have crept in at the last minute. The responsibility is entirely mine.

Some of these images are from the Computerised Local Image Collection held in Manchester Archives and Local Studies, Central Library, Manchester, M2 5PD.

The collection is made up of 77,000 images, mainly black-and-white photographs, which show the development of Manchester and the surrounding area. Strongly featured are city centre and suburban street scenes, but there are images of people, trams, Manchester at war, churches, schools and many other subjects. The whole collection can be viewed in Manchester Central Library or there is a selection on the Manchester Archives and Local Studies pages of www.manchester.gov.uk/libraries.